The Simplicity of the Gospel

VOLUME 1: GOD UNVEILED

DR. KENNETH C. BARKER

EQUIP PRESS

Colorado Springs

The Simplicity of the Gospel
Copyright © 2019 Dr. Kenneth C. Barker

All rights reserved. No part of this publication may be reproduced, distributed, or transmitted in any form or by any means, without prior written permission.

Scripture quotations marked (NIV) are taken from the Holy Bible, New International Version. Copyright © 1973, 1978, 1984, 2011 by Biblica, Inc.® Used by permission. All rights reserved worldwide.

First Edition: Year 2019
The Simplicity of the Gospel / Dr. Kenneth C. Barker
Paperback ISBN: 978-1-951304-01-0
eBook ISBN: 978-1-951304-02-7

www.simplicityofthegospel.org

Table of Contents

	Preface	5
	Introduction	10
Chapter 1	In the Beginning	12
Chapter 2	God is Creator	16
Chapter 3	God is Love	23
Chapter 4	God is Able	32
Chapter 5	God is Forgiving	38
Chapter 6	God is Redeemer	46
Chapter 7	Jesus is Savior	53
	Conclusion	59
	Glossary	60

Preface

I had the pleasure of going on a cruise with my wife last year. On the first morning of the cruise, my wife and I were on our way to the dining room for a much anticipated, restful, relaxing breakfast, prepared by someone else. As we arrived at the dining room, we were met by a closed door and another passenger who was on a similar quest. We found we were at the wrong dining room. The three of us then made our way, this time, to the correct location. As we walked, seeking the new location and anticipating the feast ahead of us, I invited the young lady to sit with us for breakfast.

During the approximately one and a half hour, breakfast, one of the many conversations we had focused on her short experience with attending church. In her entire life she had been to church on two occasions. The last time was a couple of years ago when she was visiting an aunt. The fact that she had attended church two times during her 19-year life was not what stumped me. What stumped me, or put another way, what smacked me like a brick across my face, was the response she gave when I asked about her experience at the church service. Her response came across very candid, with no malice, unaccusatory, and with all sincerity. She simply said, **"I did not understand what they were saying"**.

Over the next few minutes, she gave example after example of things, as believers, we take for granted. It hit me that as believers we have a lingo all to ourselves, and to the onlooker or the person visiting our services for the first time, that others do not understand. In our regular conversations with others and even from the pulpit on any given Sunday, "Christian Lingo" flows from our mouths like water over a waterfall, without any real thought as to where the water falls, or whether we are understood by those who seek to understand.

After this conversation, I pondered some of the words and terminologies we use on a regular basis without much thought: sanctification, justification,

Holy Spirit, God, Jesus Christ, Messiah, give life to Christ, repentance, sin, baptism, believer, disciple, grace and faith were a few that immediately came to mind. What is it like for a new person, pre-believer—the state where an individual is seeking knowledge prior to believing what he/she hears—sitting in our churches, hearing all these words that they may or may not have heard before?

This work is the first of several pieces aimed to explain these and many other concepts in as simple a manner as I can. The purpose of communication, I am reminded, is to get a message across. If the words we use do not do the trick, or if the words we use need to be defined to facilitate understanding, then my purpose is to simplify Christianity for the good of those we have wronged because of our lingo. In other words, making the gospel simple: **"The Simplicity of the Gospel"**.

I can already anticipate receiving many emails, responses, and calls challenging this and other works. My response to those challenges will be simple; this is not intended to be a doctoral dissertation, thesis, or any form of academic writing where I back the things I write about by invoking the spirits of past or present theologians and biblical scholars. If that is what you are looking for, it might be a good time to put down this work and take a class in theology or purchase an additional book that will fulfill that need. This work is not intended for you. However, if you are an individual seeking a simplistic explanation of our faith and "the hope that lies within us", I strongly suggest you continue reading.

I truly believe this, and future works of this nature, will enhance your knowledge of the Christian walk and your understanding of the hope we have in the Christ. I also pray, asking God that as you read, He will give you the ability to understand these words on paper. More importantly, I pray He will help you grow to a depth of understanding that allows you to have a closer relationship with Him. AMEN.

Dr. Kenneth C. Barker, PhD
Senior Pastor
Shepherd's Community Church
A congregation of
Grace Communion International.

The Simplicity of the Gospel:
God Unveiled

BY
DR. KENNETH C. BARKER

Introduction

Central to the life of a Christian is the belief upon which our lives are based. This belief influences our thoughts, words, deeds, and passions. We live it, breath it, are motivated by it. It dictates our mission in life, how we conduct ourselves in the workplace and at home, how we interact with each other and even the thoughts we entertain. So important is this belief that we willingly give up our lives for it. History and even our modern day, are strewn with thousands of examples of Christians who were killed and are being killed for the belief we hold. What is this belief that motivates us and for which we willingly give our lives? That belief is our belief in God.

The belief of the Christian is established upon whom we know to be the one, true, and only God. There is only one God and this one and only true God is central to the beliefs and principles to which the Christian's life hinges. To remove God is to remove our purpose for living, worshipping, and being. Without God there is no purpose to life.

This piece of work, *The Simplicity of the Gospel: The Unveiling of God*, provides a basic understanding of who God is and what His desire for you is. At first, one may question whether it is possible to know what God's desire for you is. As we go further in this work, we will see that it is possible to know the will of God. We will also see that many of the things we have heard from people about God, some of which you may have already assumed and attributed to Him, just are not true.

You will also notice that I have included a short list of words with a short definition or description of what a Christian might mean by these words. This list will be at the beginning of each chapter. To Christians, these are common words. For others, these words may need some clarification. In our communication, we often take for granted that others are knowledgeable of what we are speaking. In fact, many may not be aware of the meanings of these words. My desire is that when any of these words are used in a chapter, they will first be identified and defined in the beginning of the chapter for an added a degree of clarity. I hope this will be helpful to you. At the end of this book there is also a list of all of the "Christian words" that are used in the book. As I am only human, I may miss a few and beg your forgiveness for that.

When you read, whether you know God or do not know Him, whether you pray or don't know how to pray, periodically take some time to say just these few words. "God, help me to understand". In whatever manner you see fit, in your own words send up this request, "God help me to understand". It is only through Him that we can understand who He is and what His will is. Also, at various times during these works I will "Pause" and give you a couple of seconds or minutes to ask, "God, help me to understand". You are also free at any time to interrupt your reading and make the request as you see fit. Know that, and remember, God is the one revealing Himself to you. If at any time you do not understand what is being said, stop and send up the request, "God, help me to understand". After the request to God to help your understanding, see what happens.

"May God add a blessing to the reading of this work".

Chapter 1
In the Beginning

Christian: *One who has accepted the death of Jesus the Christ as payment for sins and has also accepted Him as his or her Lord and Master. This person is also in covenant to live a life that is in obedience to God.*

Bible: *It is believed that the Bible is comprised of many different sacred writings. Each of these sacred writings were written by men who were inspired by God over the period of centuries. This is the book that defines the Christian's way of life.*

God: *The one who has always existed. The one who created everything that exists. Without beginning or end. He is the most powerful being in existence anywhere.*

Word of God: *Is a reference to Jesus and, in some cases, a reference to the words he has spoken.*

Scriptural references: *This is an example of a notation that shows a specific part of the Bible to which we are referring. For example, John 1:2 refers to the first chapter in the book of John and the second verse.*

The Christian believes the Bible is the written word of God. There are many who question the authority of the Bible and whether it is truly the word of God. In a later book I will address this issue, but for now we will assume the Bible is the word of God. We will also assume God inspired men to write these words on scrolls or parchments and these writings were kept safely for hundreds of years. These works were placed into one great work we now know as and call the Bible. This is the work containing the instructions for Christian belief and living.

> *John 1:1-2 In the beginning was the Word, and the Word was with God, and the Word was God. ² He was in the beginning with God.*

There are many questions about the beginning and the "origin" of God that have been asked through time. Questions such as:

1. When was the beginning? How long ago are we talking about?
2. Did God have a beginning?
3. Did God always exist?
4. Who made God?

These are fair questions. Our minds lead us to question things we do not really understand or things that do not appear to fall within what we consider normal. In order to understand the answers to these and similar questions, it is helpful to recognize that the matter on which we live and the matter we are made up of will decay. The human being and all that is around us is subject to decay. As such, our thinking has been influenced by the reality that the physical things are temporary. We look around us and everything decays and dies. All living things are subject to decay and death. Decay and dying can also be witnessed in the non-living world. For example, concrete, when exposed to the elements, is subject to decay. And, though some steel can take up to 500 years to break down, it will eventually break down.

Our typical and limited human thinking is based on the belief that there is always a beginning and an end. As difficult as it is, I ask you to set aside our thoughts that all things have a beginning and an end, as that concept does not apply to God.

==PAUSE==

==REFLECT==

God does not have a beginning or an end. He always was, always is, and will always be. God is not subject to our time. With God, *"A thousand years in your sight are like a day that has just gone by"* (Psalm 90:4). When the Christian speaks about God as being "eternal" or "everlasting", we are referring to God as not having a beginning or an end. God has lived forever and will continue to live forever. There is not a beginning nor an end for God.

In the book of John 1:1 and 2, it talks about two beings existing in the beginning. But when you think about the beginning, however far back that may be, the question comes, "Well what existed before that point of time we call the beginning?" Again, our human limitations cannot think in terms of a time frame that is prior to the beginning.

Psalms 90:2 talks about God existing *"from everlasting to everlasting"* and compares God's existence to the frail and short-lived existence of man. It talks about man being returned to the dust. I have found it easier to accept my human limitation and view the limitlessness of the existence of God as one of those things that is beyond my understanding at this time.

== PAUSE==

==REFLECT==

I also view this as a WOW moment. WOW, how awesome is our God that He has always existed? WOW, how awesome it is to have lived all that time and what wisdom must He have gained along the way (assuming, as some do, that God learns)? As human beings, we look at our grandparents and for those who are fortunate enough, great grandparents, and admire the great wisdom they have accumulated over the 70, 80, 90, or even 100 years they have been alive.

We honor such a life full of wisdom and experiences. How much more can we honor the life of God who has always lived? WOW, how much can I learn from this individual? How many pitfalls can I avoid if I tap into such a vast pool of knowledge? After all, He has seen, observed and interacted with man from the beginning of man's existence on this earth—WOW.

The main takeaway from this chapter is that God is not limited by the time that man has established. We measure time based on the spin of the earth that gives us the day and the orbit of the earth around the sun that gives us our year. The Christian believes that God does not exist within this time measurement system and, therefore, He is not governed by it. We believe He created all things (the topic of Chapter 2), including the earth and sun by which we measure our time. It is safe to say that God existed before time began.

If you find it necessary, please feel free to re-read this chapter. Remember to "pause", take some time and soak it in prior to moving on to Chapter 2, where you will be reading about "God is Creator".

Chapter 2
God is Creator

Creation Week: *The segment of time within which God the Creator, created all things. This period is divided into 7 segments identified in the Bible as days. As there are 7 days in which God created, this segment of time became known as Creation Week.*

Creator: *Refers to the one who created all things. The Christian refers to this person as God.*

Living Thing: *Any organism that has been "birthed", grows, feeds, has the ability to reproduce, and eventually dies.*

> *Revelation 4:11 You are worthy, our Lord and God, to receive glory and honor and power, for you created all things, and by your will they were created and have their being.*

The theory of *Intelligent Design*, purports that life, or the universe, cannot have arisen by chance. This theory states that life, or the universe, was designed and created by some intelligent entity. The theory of intelligent design holds that certain features of the universe and of living things are best explained by an intelligent cause, not an undirected process such as natural selection.

Intelligent design does not argue for or against a creationist view of life. Intelligent design simply utilizes the evidence available to determine whether the "apparent design" in nature is the result of an intelligent cause, or the result of an undirected process such as natural selection.

Christians believe living things did not come out of nothingness, especially when we consider the order that exists in all life forms. Each species reproducing after its own kind, this is intelligent design. Intelligent design is the reason we do not have fish giving birth to monkeys or lizards giving birth to birds, or cows giving birth to humans. We believe that intelligent design is factual, that there is intelligent design in all life forms. We believe there is an intelligent being who established this design and the order we observe. This intelligent designer is God.

In Chapter One, we talked about God as always existing. In the beginning was God. At whatever point we believe man's history began, God was there. I hope that you are beginning to see the enormity of a being that has always existed. In this chapter, we will see that God, who has always existed, has a purpose. His purpose is what He has been involved in throughout eternity. Right now, you may be thinking, "That's a long time to be around. Does he not become bored? Does he not become tired doing what he does over those millions of years?"

As a mental health professional, I have had the opportunity to speak with many people about their lives, the challenges they face, and their motivation for staying the course. Through these many sessions, as well as much reading and research in the area of human behavior, I have no doubt that there is a large gap between those who want to "throw in the towel" and give up, and those, who after many years of trials and failures, are still motivated to keep moving forward. I have also found that, invariably, the difference between those who want to continue and those who want to quit, is purpose.

Having a purpose in life gives us focus, gives meaning such that even though things may not be going entirely as we have planned, we are still driven. God has a purpose. Genesis 1:1 states, "In the beginning God created the heavens and the earth."

When the Christian speaks about or refers to the Creator, we are referring to God, who has always existed, creating everything we see, hear, and experience.

In Genesis 1:1 it states that He created the heavens and the earth. Consider for a moment the heavens and all this entails. A brief internet search will show that the estimated diameter of our observable universe is approximately 93 billion light years across. Put simply, it is the distance that light will travel in 93 billion years. This universe, it is estimated, contains more than 100 billion galaxies. In our galaxy, the Milky Way, it is estimated there are close to 30 billion planets. One of these planets is called Earth. Take a moment and "PAUSE".

==PAUSE==

==REFLECT==

Consider our planet earth. The earth is 7,917 miles in diameter and 24,901 miles in circumference at the equator, turning on its axis at a rate of 1,000 miles per hour. On this earth, which can easily be considered "infinitely insignificant" (my terminology) when compared to the size of this universe, God chose to create. He had already created the heavens and all its celestial bodies, and He created the earth.

Then we have what we refer to as Creation Week. I would like to pause here for a minute to let you know that even among Christians there is some debate as to whether it was a literal seven days or whether the seven days in the creation account represent a longer time period. My purpose is not to debate on this issue but to make Christianity simple. Whether He took seven days, seven weeks, months, years, centuries, or millions of years is truly irrelevant at this point. What is important is that God created. Creation Week refers to the time God took to create everything we see.

As you read this next section, I want to encourage you, if you have a Bible, to keep it handy so that you can read about the account of the creation while you go through this next section. If you do not have a Bible, you should be able to read along using an online version, or just go to one of the search engines and type in "Genesis 1".

When you begin your search for a Bible, you will find there is quite a selection of versions to choose from. Without getting into all of the who, when, where, why, and how, I suggest the New King James (NKJ) or the New International Version (NIV).

==PAUSE==

==REFLECT==

The Bible is divided into books, chapters, and verses. This format is used to reference any specific place in the Bible that you may choose to read. For example, if we were to choose Genesis 1:1, this would mean we are reading the Book of Genesis, Chapter 1, Verse 1. Most Bibles, toward the front, would have a list of all of the books in the Bible with the page number where that book begins. Go to the page number where the book of Genesis begins.

Next, we find the chapter. The first number that appears after the book's name designates the chapter of the book we will be reading. In this case, Genesis 1:1, the first number after the book's name "Genesis" is "1". We will be reading from the first chapter of the book of Genesis. The chapters are designated by the large, bolded numbers that appear throughout the book.

Next, is the verse of the chapter we will be reading. The verses are identified by the numbers which appear within the text of the chapter. With the exception of the first verse, all other verses are identified by a number. In Genesis 1:1, the number appearing immediately after the colon is "1". This is the first verse in the chapter. This verse begins immediately after the chapter number. You will not find the number one. All verses after the first verse will be designated with a number.

On Genesis, find the page where the book of Genesis begins. Chapter 1, the large, bold number one (1), designates the first chapter of the book of Genesis. Verse "1", is the first verse of the chapter designated by the smaller number that appears immediately after the colon. This is where we begin reading.

What we refer to as Creation Week is the time that God took to create all that we see on this earth. The following is the account of the time period as recorded in the book of Genesis:

Genesis 1:1-5	Day 1	*God created the heavens and the earth; he created light and called it day and the darkness he called night.*
Genesis 1:6-8	Day 2	*He created light called it day and darkness he called night.*
Genesis 1:9-13	Day 3	*God created the atmosphere, grass, herbs, trees, fruit and vegetation. He created them with the ability to reproduce.*
Genesis 1:14-19	Day 4	*God created the sun to give light during the day and the moon to give light at night.*
Genesis 1:20-23	Day 5	*He created everything that lives in the waters and that flies above the earth: Fish, whales, birds...*
Genesis 1:24-25	Day 6	*God made all beasts of the field, cattle and all animals that walk upon the earth. On Day 6 God also made man and woman. God gave animals and humanity the ability to reproduce. God gave humanity authority over all that he had created.*
Genesis 2:1-2	Day 7	*On this 7th day, God rested.*

Everything we see on the earth and in the heavens is as a result of God. Every law of nature we observe is because of God. We do not wonder who set the laws in motion because God was careful to tell us that He did it. He created every living thing with the ability to reproduce living things like themselves. This is the reason you cannot plant an orange tree and get an apple. It is the same reason man reproduces after his kind and why a woman and man coming together in a sexual relation has a human baby and not a calf. This is the reason that cats have kittens, dogs have puppies, and rocks do not reproduce. God created and established in His creation a prescribed order of the way things work.

==PAUSE==

("GOD, HELP ME TO PROCESS THIS")

As human beings, we are subject to imperfections. One of the imperfections we experience is the ability to forget. We forget our keys. We forget our glasses. On some occasions, if you are anything like me, you may even forget your children's names. It is just one of those things. Unfortunately, many times we also forget who God is and that it is He who has created us.

Though we may forget God, we are always on His mind. Isn't it interesting that even before He created man on the earth — Day 6 — He took the time to plan everything that will be necessary for your survival and for our life? He took the time and created water, air, and food; He took the time to design our digestive system in such a way that it digests the things designed for our consumption. He designed our respiratory system in such a way that we can breathe air and not water like a fish. He created us with a brain that controls all human functions and a mind that can use information, manipulate our surroundings, and adapt to changes.

Then, "God saw all that He had made, and it was very good" (Genesis

1:31). After a period of creating, I can imagine God sitting back, relaxing and looking at all that He had made. I can imagine the satisfaction He felt when He surveyed what He had made and then said, "Yes. That's awesome." I am sure you also experienced something similar.

I love working with my hands. I love building things. After every project, I just sit for a few minutes and take it in. I soak in the pleasures that are derived from a job well done. Much in the same way, but I guess on a much larger scale, God did the same. He looked at humanity, animals, trees, plants, birds, fish, and celestial bodies and He enjoyed what He had made. God made you. He made you. He created you, looked upon you, and said, "You are very good" (Genesis 1:31).

==PAUSE==

("GOD, LET ME SEE ME THE WAY YOU SEE ME.")

If you find it necessary, please feel free to re-read this chapter. And remember to "pause", take some time, and soak it in prior to moving on to Chapter 3, where you will be reading about "God is Love".

Chapter 3
God is Love

Messiah: *From the Hebrew language, the Messiah refers to the promised deliverer of the Jewish nation prophesied in the Hebrew sacred writings. The Christian believes the word Messiah is the title of the one who is the promised deliverer of all who seeks delivery. Jesus is a common name of God who became man. Jesus is regarded by Christians as the Messiah or Savior of the Hebrew prophecies and the savior of humanity.*

> *1 John 4:16 And so we know and rely on the love God has for us. God is love. Whoever lives in love lives in God, and God in them.*

In our society, there are many songs written on the topic of love and infatuation. These songs are about the love that occurs between a man and a woman. As typical love songs go, they try to put into words the beliefs, feelings, and emotions experienced by individuals who are in love. These songs attempt to describe the euphoric feelings experienced by individuals who are in love.

We say that "God is love". But what does this mean? If you ask 50 people what love is, you will receive 50 different answers. It appears love is one of those things that you know what it looks like, you know how it "feels", but you have a difficult time putting the proper words together that will accurately describe love in the manner and in the context you would like.

For example: I love hotdogs, I love my wife, I love my kids, I love my mother, and I love sports. I dare say that though these statements are all true, the love I share with my wife is far different from the love I have for hot dogs, or the love I have for my mother or sports. Though all of these are considered love, I would still have a difficult time defining in words what love is.

In the English language we are limited to just a few words that may describe or define love. In the Greek language there are six words that describe love. Four of them are used in various places in the Bible. I will first describe the six Greek words and then I will give an example of where four of them can be found in the Bible.

First, *Eros*. This love was named after the Greek god of fertility. It is the romantic or sexual love experienced by a man and a woman within the bonds of marriage and ordained by God. It is an erotic love by which sexual passion and desire are expressed.

The second is *Philia*. This is the love you will have toward a friend. It is based on the deep comradery that develops between individuals who fight together on the battlefield. *Philia* is about loyalty, sacrifice, and the sharing of emotions. The city of Philadelphia is known as the City of Brotherly Love for this same reason. The name of the city is derived from the Greek word *Philia*.

The third is *Ludus*. This is a playful type of love. Often, Ludus, can be witnessed when siblings interact together in a playful "loving" manner. We also may have seen or experienced this kind of love in situations where flirting and playful teasing occur during the early stages of a relationship.

The fourth, *Agape*, is a selfless love. It is a love for everyone, regardless. This love is extended to family members, friends, strangers, co-workers, and even enemies. This form of love is considered in the Christian community as the highest form of love. This is the type of love that leads us to care for strangers. It allows us to reach out to someone in need even though we may not know who they are or where they are from. This is a love that has no conditions. This love loves just because and for no reason.

The fifth, *Pragma*, is a longstanding love. It is a love that is often found among individuals who have shared each other's company for years. This love is often found in couples who have been married for many years. In such cases, the *Eros* may have long been absent from the relationship; however, these couples still have *Pragma* for each other. *Pragma* is about giving love rather than receiving love.

The sixth, *Philautia*, is the love of one's self. There is the unhealthy narcissism *Philautia*, which focuses on self-obsession and personal gratification. The is also the healthy form of *Philautia*, which emphasizes loving yourself to the degree you will have enough love and security to give to others.

==PAUSE==

("GOD, HELP ME TO UNDERSTAND LOVE")

Examples of all these forms of love can be seen in the pages of the Bible. Each of these forms, within the right context, are appropriate and encouraged by God. For example:

Eros can be seen in 1 Corinthians 7:8-9 when the Apostle Paul, speaking to young Christians, stated, *"Now to the unmarried and the widows I say: It is good for them to stay unmarried, as I do. ⁹ But if they cannot control themselves, they should marry, for it is better to marry than to burn with passion."*

Philia	1 Thessalonians 4:9	*"Now about your love for one another we do not need to write to you, for you yourselves have been taught by God to love each other."*
Agape	John 13:34-35	*"A new command I give you: Love one another. As I have loved you, so you must love one another. ³⁵ By this everyone will know that*

Pragma	Matthew 18:19	*you are my disciples, if you love one another."* *"Again I say unto you, That if two of you shall agree on earth as touching any **thing** that they shall ask, it shall be done for them of my Father which is in heaven."* The word "thing" in this verse is the Greek word *Pragma* which refers to anything done in an act of love towards another.

Now that you have a better grasp of love, we will look at the love that God has for us. Much like a human being who has a baby for the purpose of cuddling, loving, caring, protecting, and providing for it, so, too, did God create humanity for the purpose of having a relationship with us. God loves us (1 John 4:9-10).

In Chapters 1 and 2, you saw that God had always existed and He created. On the sixth "day of creation", God created humanity. As a demonstration of His love, He did not create man first. Had He done this, man may not have survived, or at best, man's existence would have been extremely uncomfortable. God, in His loving wisdom, created all that was necessary for man's survival and existence on the earth.

God created the air we breathe, food we eat, and even set in motion laws of nature and the cycle of life. It is a sustaining cycle that allows trees to continue to bear fruit, fish and animals to continue to reproduce, and vegetables to continue to be produced, all for man's benefit.

Man was given a beautiful garden, Eden, to live in, and he had a one-on-one, personal relationship with God. God had walks in the garden of Eden where Adam and Eve lived, Genesis 3:8. God, because of His love, gave man the privilege of naming all the animals. He also gave him dominion over everything that lived on the face of the earth. Everything he ever needed was available to him through God. That is a lot of favor shown to man.

There are multiple times during the history of humanity that man has hurt, disappointed, betrayed, and disrespected God. During these times, God still loved, while man was the one that stepped away from the relationship. Every time man broke the relationship with God, God never gave up on humanity, but pursued us.

The Bible, from the first book, Genesis, to the last, Revelation, is a story about a relationship. It is a relationship between God and humanity. God pursues a relationship with humanity and man is unfaithful, disobedient, and disrespectful to God. Throughout the pages of the Bible, humanity and Israel have continually lived contrary to the law of God. Man, because of his choices, receives the consequences for his actions. He then cries out to God for deliverance and God forgives, redeems, and restores him. It does not take man long to forget God and return to the same way of life that led to his separation from God.

Because of the limited time and space, it will take to go through all the circumstances where man turned his back on God, and God forgave and restored, I will give a summary. The next few paragraphs will highlight this on and mostly off relationship.

The first man, Adam, and his wife, Eve, were given specific instructions by God. Adam and Eve were allowed to eat from any tree in the garden except for one tree. The tree of Knowledge of Good and Evil (Genesis 2:15-17). They disobeyed, ate, and then tried to hide their sin. They even tried to lie to God about it. Later, Cain killed his brother Abel in a fit of anger (Genesis 4:8). Society deteriorated to the point where God was sorry that He had made man on the earth and God was grieved to His heart (Genesis 6:6).

So much was this deterioration that God destroyed the world by flood, except for the family of Noah (Genesis 6-9). Civilization continued to get worse even after the flood and several incidents occurred that were the result of sin in the lives of those God had created.

The world took a turn for the worse and God called Abram and told him to go to a place that God would show him and out of him God would make a great nation (Genesis 12). In Genesis 17:5, God changed Abram's name to Abraham and his descendants were the children of Israel. Israel was enslaved to the Egyptians (1523 BC – 1313 BC) and cried out to God for deliverance (Exodus 3:9), and God delivered them (Exodus 12:51).

Because of their sin and disobedience to the ways of God, Israel was allowed to be taken into captivity by King Nebuchadnezzar into Babylon (423 – 372 BC), then the Persians/Medians (372 – 348 BC), and Greece (371 - 140 BC). Each time the children of Israel cried out to God for deliverance and He forgave and delivered.

Israel was a rebellious land with people who did not follow nor obey God regarding everything He said. After God delivered them from the captivity of the Egyptians, they complained and longed to go back to Egypt. Some of the Israelites even returned to their Egyptian captors. Personally, I believe it to be ungrateful when someone is rescued and after being rescued, they turn around and return their captors. But God continually forgives and restores because of the love He has for His people.

Time and time again Israel, like us, rebelled against the ways of God, but God still loves. Like Adam and Eve, we have choices and often we choose to take of the "tree of the knowledge of good and evil". Making the choice to take from this tree is the same as us making our own decisions as to what is right and what is wrong. We decide for ourselves what we choose to do much like the Israelites. Much like the Israelites, when we go before God, He is willing and quick to forgive all because of the love He has for us.

God's love is so immense and far reaching that the Word — the one who had been with God *"In the Beginning"* (John 1:1), *"became flesh and dwelt among us"* (John 1:14). He was the one who became Jesus the Christ/

Messiah/Savior. Because of the love He has for us, He came to this earth as a human. Because of His love for us, He lived a life of suffering (Isaiah 53:3). Because of His love for us, He suffered a grueling and painful punishment (John 19). Because of His love, He suffered humiliation (Luke 22:63-65). Because of His love for us, He willingly died on the cross (Luke 23:33) so that our sins can be forgiven (1 Peter 3:18). *"For God so loved the world, that he gave his one and only son, that whoever believes in him will not perish but have eternal life"* (John 3:16).

And finally, as the Apostle Paul stated in Romans 8:38-39, *"For I am convinced that neither death nor life, neither angels nor demons, neither the present nor the future, nor any powers, ^{39} neither height nor depth, nor anything else in all creation, will be able to separate us from the love of God that is in Christ Jesus our Lord"*.

God is love. God loves. He has created us for a loving relationship with Him. I now ask, "Do you have a relationship with Him?" Is there anything that stands in the way of you having that relationship with Him? Sometimes people believe that the things they have done are not worthy of forgiveness and that God will not forgive. I hope by now you have seen that there is nothing that can stand between you and God unless you allow it.

"Here I am! I stand at the door and knock. If anyone hears my voice and opens the door, I will come in and eat with that person, and they with me" (Revelation 3:20). Even right now as you read, you may be experiencing an urging towards God. Do not neglect or ignore this movement of the Holy Spirit. This is God calling to you. He is knocking.

If you are experiencing this urge now and you are not sure what to do, I am going to offer a suggestion.

1. Take this book with you.
2. Go right now and find a quiet place where you can be alone with God.

3. Say the following prayer:

   "Lord God. I have sinned and my life has strayed from the path you desired. I am sorry for the wrong I have done, please forgive me. I want to live a life that is pleasing to you. Help me do so. Help me to surrender my life to your will. In Jesus' name I pray, Amen."

This prayer does not save us. Only Jesus can, as we saw earlier. This prayer is intended to help you "break the ice" with God. It is your continued walk with God that helps you build and develop a relationship with him. As you grow in relationship with God you will speak with Him using your own prayers.

4. Seek out a group of believers in your community. Here is one place Google can be helpful.

==PAUSE==

(GOD, HELP ME UNDERSTAND THE DEPTHS OF YOUR LOVE FOR ME)

God's love for us is so deep, and broad, wide, and unexplainable that even today He makes provisions for us. Even today, in this "modern" age, because God still expects His creations — humanity — to live righteous lives, He has given us a helper. Holy Spirit is that helper that is available to "guide us into all truth" (John 6:13); to intercede before God on our behalf when we fall short; and to also intercede on our behalf when we do wrong (Romans 8:26).

God making the Holy Spirit available to us is a demonstration of His love toward us. In the beginning, God created because of His love. Throughout history, God has demonstrated His love to humanity by way of all He did on our behalf. Even today, He continues to participate in the lives of those who believe in Him and obey Him. Undoubtedly, he will continue to do the same in the future.

==PAUSE==

(GOD, HOW ARE YOU PARTICIPATING WITH ME)

---------------- **Chapter 4** ----------------

God is Able

Amen: *It is a word said by all Christians at the end of every prayer. It symbolizes our agreement with what was said during the prayer.*

Christ: *Messiah or savior. It is a title given to Jesus as He is the savior of humanity. Christians use this title when referring to Jesus.*

Church: *Comes from the Greek work Ekklesia meaning called out ones. Referring to the people or followers of the Christian God. This word "Church" does not refer to a "Church Building" but to the people.*

Jesus: *the common name that was given to the Messiah or Savior when He was born. It is the common name given to God when He lived in the flesh. Christians use this name in reference to the Messiah.*

Live your life for Christ: *Living in obedience to everything God says. Living a life in total submission to God.*

> *Ephesians 3:20-21 Now to him who is able to do immeasurably more than all we ask or imagine, according to his power that is at work within us, to him be glory in the church and in Christ Jesus throughout all generations, for ever and ever! Amen.*

In Chapter 2 you learned that God is Creator. Though in this short body of work it is impossible to explore the vast expanse of what He has created, I am sure you've gotten the gist of what He is able to do. When we consider all that He has already done, is there any doubt that He is capable of a lot more. He is the one who has created ALL things in the heavens. When we look up into the sky at night, we only get a small glimpse into what He has created. When we look upon the earth and examine what He has done we only get a sneak preview of what He is capable of.

There is an old song by Charles Crozat Converse titled, "What a Friend We Have in Jesus". In one of the verses there are the words, "Oh what peace we often forfeit, oh what needless pain we bear. All because we do not carry, everything to God in prayer". So much more can be accomplished for us and by us if we will only ask God, who is able. It is unfortunate that for various reasons we do not ask. James 4:2-3 explains, *"You desire but do not have, so you kill. You covet but you cannot get what you want, so you quarrel and fight. You do not have because you do not ask God.*[3] *When you ask, you do not receive, because you ask with wrong motives, that you may spend what you get on your pleasures."*

Ephesians 3:20-21 says, *"Now to him who is able to do immeasurably more than all we ask or imagine, according to his power that is at work within us,*[21] *to him be glory in the church and in Christ Jesus throughout all generations, for ever and ever! Amen."* This scripture indicates to us that God can do quite a bit. Immeasurably — unable to be measured — above all that you can ask or think. I don't know about you, but I can imagine quite a lot. The capacity of our God to give, help, share, protect, provide, heal, encourage, comfort, support, counsel … is far above anything we can imagine.

CAUTION

Please do not take this to mean that God will automatically give to us anything we ask for. Many new believers wrongfully apply this scripture to mean that anything I want or desire, God is compelled to give it simply because we ask. Yes, God can give us the desires of our hearts; however, the purpose of this chapter is just to show you what God is capable of. There are times He may choose not to fulfill our hearts' desires, only because He knows what is best. For now, just knowing what He is capable of, I pray, is enough to give you hope.

On a grand scale, there are examples of the works of God that demonstrate He is truly able. We can also see what He is capable of on a much smaller scale and within the lives of individuals. Throughout my life, I have seen example after example of God showing He is able. As you live your life for Christ — live lives based on what God's desires are — you will begin to see examples of His abilities in the lives of individuals, if you have not already begun to see and experience these occurrences.

I love telling stories about what God can do, and there are quite a few. One I love telling is of the time I was 18 years old. I am sure that you are aware that eighteen-year-olds take quite a few risks. I did things without even considering the consequences. One time, I was riding at the back of a flatbed truck. The truck driver slowed to make a sharp right turn to get onto a bridge. This bridge was not paved, and the surface was composed of dirt and was very bumpy. As the truck slowed, I jumped off the back with the intention of running across the dried river bed, and making my way up the opposite bank where I would then jump back into the bed of the truck.

All was going fine. I jumped off the bed of the truck. Ran down the near bank of the river and across its dried bed. I propelled myself up the opposite bank. Proud of my quick and agile accomplishment, I stood on the other side of the bridge awaiting the truck so that I could jump back into the bed. At this point, the driver of the flatbed truck saw me and, anticipating what was about to happen, he placed his foot quite suddenly and quite heavily on the accelerator pedal of the truck. This led to a chain of event that dramatically increased the velocity of the truck. The speed of the truck, coupled with the many large bumps on the bridge, led the truck to suddenly go airborne. There

I was. Standing in front of a two-ton, airborne truck. And there I was, picking myself up from the dried river bed below. What happened?

I can only give the honor to God, who is able. This conclusion was further solidified when I finally got into the truck. I looked at the driver and it was as though he had seen a ghost. A black man who looked like all the blood had drained from his face. His face was pale, jaw dropped, and I could notably see his body shaking. As he forced the words through his lips the words were, "Where did you go?" As we talked about the incident from his perspective, he "slammed" on the accelerator to leave me behind. The truck went airborne and out of control. One second, he saw me in front of the truck's grill. He swore the truck was going to hit me. Then I disappeared. God is able.

I can tell the story of a friend of mine. He and his wife were sitting in their kitchen. She had taken the last can of baked beans out of the cabinet and prepared it for their dinner. They sat at the dinner table and prayed. Firstly, giving thanks to God for the blessing of that last meal they had. During the prayer he also prayed that God would continue to be faithful to them in providing additional meals. Before they were too much into the meal, there was a knock on the front door. At the door was someone who presented him with a sealed envelope. She said that God told her to come to their house and drop off the envelope she had prepared. After expressing much thanks, he returned to the dinner table where his wife and his half-finished plate of baked beans were awaiting. Propelled by curiosity, he eagerly opened the envelope and emptied its contents. He looked, and there, laying in his hand was a check in the amount of $150.00. God is able.

As I write, I also remember one elderly lady in my congregation. She had been admitted to the hospital because of a condition for which the doctors did not know the cause. During a visit to the hospital, I took the time to comfort and pray with her. She became much more relaxed and soon fell asleep. The next day, I got a call from her excited daughter. I have never heard such a combination of words before. The words were put together in the following order: "The Doctor said that mommy does not have diabetes anymore." Wow. I have heard a lot of things, but I have never heard of someone not having diabetes anymore. God is able.

Maybe you can think of specific times in your life where God was present and God showed you He was able. Where He came to the rescue. Where you were out of hope with no chance of improving your situation, and just then things took a turn for the better. It is not always a life and death situation. Sometimes it is simply someone coming along to help you out of a difficult situation.

One time, the one-ton truck I was driving got stuck way out in the middle of nowhere. I tried to get it out of the sand, but it only sank deeper. I prayed and asked God for help. Within less than five minutes, a gentleman just "happened" to be driving by on that road, and he "happened" to have a winch. God is able.

God is so able that sometimes He prepares for what we will need long before the need arises or before we even ask. He had prepared this gentleman with his winch that day and directed him to take that dirt road just so that he could have an encounter with me and save me from the sand. Rescue was on the way before I had even asked and even prior to the truck being stuck in the sand. Scripture talks about God knowing what we need before we even ask, *"… for your Father knows what you need before you ask him"* (Matthew 6:8).

Quite often we tend not to give much thought to these occurrences and assume them to be coincidences. Yes, they may be coincidences, however, they are coincidences that are instigated and followed through to the end by our God. They are incidences where God allows His answer to our prayers to develop at the same time the situation from which we need deliverance occurs. He is our creator who cares deeply for us and undoubtedly there has been at least one instance during your life when God stepped in and saved you. He is able.

Take a few moments and think back to one of those instances. If you have difficulty remembering, ask God to help you remember. He was there when it happened, and He will help you.

==PAUSE==

("GOD, SHOW ME WHERE YOU HAVE BEEN ABLE IN MY LIFE")

There is nothing that can happen in your life that God cannot handle. Who do you need God to be in your life? Do you need Him to be a comforter? He said, "I am."

Do you need Him to be a provider? He said, "I am."

Do you need Him to be a comforter during times of turmoil? He said, "I am."

Or, maybe you need Him to be a guide as you navigate troubled waters. He said, "I am."

What is it that you may be struggling with in your life right now? Is there something that you need help with? What are the challenges that you are faced with right now? Is your challenge to find a purpose for your life? Or, is the challenge to cope with the regular mundane things of your life? Take a few minutes now and PAUSE.

==PAUSE==

("GOD, WHERE IN MY LIFE DO I NEED YOU?")

If you find it necessary, please feel free to re-read this chapter. And remember to "pause", take some time, and soak it in prior to moving on to Chapter 5, where you will be reading about "God is Forgiving".

Chapter 5
God is Forgiving

Garden of Eden: *The place where God put Adam and Eve to live after he created them.*

Adam: *The first man created by God. He was created from dirt.*

Eve: *The first woman created by God. She was created from the rib of her husband Adam.*

The Serpent: *Symbolic reference to Satan. First referenced in the book of Genesis as the one who tempted Eve.*

Tree of Knowledge of Good and Evil: *A symbolic or literal tree from which God forbade Adam and Eve from taking its fruit.*

Lord: *Title given to God as Master of all.*

> *Micah 7:18-19 Who is a God like you, who pardons sin and forgives the transgression of the remnant of his inheritance? You do not stay angry forever but delight to show mercy. You will again have compassion on us; you will tread our sins underfoot and hurl all our iniquities into the depths of the sea.*

God made man. As recorded in the book of Genesis, He created Adam and Eve. After Adam and Eve were created by God, God Himself took care of them. They were in want of nothing. God took care of all their needs. He gave them dominion over the fish of the sea, the birds of the air, and the animals of the land. He gave Adam and Eve a beautiful place to live. This place was called the Garden of Eden. Man had free dominion over everything that was in the garden. Can you imagine? Not having to toil all day and night just to put some food on our tables, a roof over our heads, and clothing on our backs? Adam and Eve even had personal contact, conversations, and interactions with the one who created all the universe and all that is on the earth. Can you imagine?

==PAUSE==

("GOD, HELP ME TO IMAGINE WHAT THIS RELATIONSHIP MIGHT HAVE BEEN LIKE")

Total access and total dominion were afforded to Adam and Eve. Until, one day, it all changed. Humanity, who was created in a state of perfection and whose life was in perfect harmony with God, disobeyed God and began to live a life that was dictated by Satan. Since then, all of humanity has been under the influence of Satan and lived lives that are separate from God and contrary to the way our Creator intended. In Chapter 3 of the book of Genesis, we see an account of how this happened. What follows is the account of the incident in the Garden of Eden that led to the downfall of Adam and Eve. You can read it in your own Bible or read what follows:

> *Now the serpent was more crafty than any of the wild animals the* LORD *God had made. He said to the woman, "Did God really say, 'You must not eat from any tree in the garden'?"*
>
> *² The woman said to the serpent, "We may eat fruit from the trees in the garden, ³ but God did say, 'You must not eat fruit from the tree that is in the middle of the garden, and you must not touch it, or you will die.'"*
>
> *⁴ "You will not certainly die," the serpent said to the woman. ⁵ "For God knows that when you eat from it your eyes will be opened, and you will be like God, knowing good and evil."*

⁶ When the woman saw that the fruit of the tree was good for food and pleasing to the eye, and also desirable for gaining wisdom, she took some and ate it. She also gave some to her husband, who was with her, and he ate it. ⁷ Then the eyes of both of them were opened, and they realized they were naked; so they sewed fig leaves together and made coverings for themselves.

⁸ Then the man and his wife heard the sound of the Lord God as he was walking in the garden in the cool of the day, and they hid from the Lord God among the trees of the garden. ⁹ But the Lord God called to the man, "Where are you?"

¹⁰ He answered, "I heard you in the garden, and I was afraid because I was naked; so I hid."

¹¹ And he said, "Who told you that you were naked? Have you eaten from the tree that I commanded you not to eat from?"

¹² The man said, "The woman you put here with me—she gave me some fruit from the tree, and I ate it."

¹³ Then the Lord God said to the woman, "What is this you have done?" The woman said, "The serpent deceived me, and I ate."

God told man he could take and eat of any tree that was in the Garden of Eden except for one tree, the tree of *Knowledge of Good and Evil*. God did not withhold anything from Adam and Eve. Total dominion except for one tree. When Adam chose to take from the tree of *Knowledge of Good and Evil*, in effect, they chose for themselves what was right and what was wrong. They took it upon themselves to decide, without the guidance of their Creator, what was good and what was evil, what was right and what was wrong, what was moral and what was immoral. This is precisely what humanity is doing today. In pushing God to the side, humanity is making all of its determinations outside of the influence of God. Remember, God is the one who designed and created us and who knows the purpose for which He designed us.

This act of taking from the tree of *Knowledge of Good and Evil*, choosing for themselves what was right and wrong, was where sin first entered the world. Romans 5:12 explains, *"Therefore, just as sin entered the world through one man, and death through sin, and in this way death came to all people, because all sinned."* Sin entered the world through Adam and Eve. Because sin is now present in the world, the natural consequence or result of sin in the life of an individual is death. Death came into the world because sin came into the world. And because all have sinned, death is the result of sin in our lives.

Many individuals tend to blame Adam and Eve for the sins we commit. However, to be honest and fair to Adam and Eve, they were nowhere near me when I was doing my wrong. I am also positive that they were not around urging you along when you did the wrong that you did. Each of us is accountable for our own wrongdoing. Every one of us had the same opportunity to choose to do the right or wrong thing. We chose to do wrong. We have no one else to blame but ourselves. I know there are some who would say, "but I had no choice. If I did not do *this* then *that* would have happened." Though this may have been true, there was still a choice. We may not have liked the result, but the choice was there. Sometimes in life we must make tough choices, and sometimes there are no pleasing outcomes.

==PAUSE==

("GOD, AM I TRULY RESPONSIBLE FOR ALL THE CHOICES I MAKE?")

When we sin, we choose the way of evil, the way of the devil and in so doing reject God. When we sin, we in fact are saying to God that I value the way of evil more than I value your way. This naturally creates a separation between us and God. The more we sin, the more we reinforce this desire to be away from the presence and goodness of God.

What is it like for a parent who "gave birth" to a child, does all that he/she can for that child, and then later finds that the child chooses another way for himself, chooses another parent, and goes as far as rejecting and even denies the existence of the parent? As a parent, I will never want to experience something like that. However, this is exactly what God experiences with us when we disobey and sin and make choices that are ultimately harmful to us.

God is a good parent. He is willing to "take us back". He is willing to bridge the gap that was created between Him and us because of our sin. He is willing to forgive. Forgiveness is a voluntary process by which someone who has been wronged — God — undergoes a change in their attitude regarding an offense that was committed — sin. From the perspective of human beings, we choose to forgive and let go of negative emotions such as anger, hate, vengefulness, and, in many cases, a desire to see the offending party hurt or be punished. God is willing and ready to forgive us our sins.

In the book of Micah, the prophet asked the question, *"Who is a God like you, who pardons sin and forgives the transgression … you do not stay angry forever … you will again have compassion on us"* (Micah 7:18). Psalms 103:12 says, *"As far as the east is from the west, so far has he removed our transgressions from us"*. Daniel 9:9 says, *"The Lord our God is merciful and forgiving, even though we have rebelled against him."* God's desire to forgive us for the sins we have committed is based on the love He still has for those He created.

Nowhere in the Bible is the forgiveness of God so exemplified as in the story of the prodigal son. This story is found in the Book of Luke, 15:11-32. Again, please feel free to read it in your own Bible or follow:

Jesus continued: "There was a man who had two sons. ^{12} The younger one said to his father, 'Father, give me my share of the estate.' So he divided his property between them.

^{13} "Not long after that, the younger son got together all he had, set off for a distant country and there squandered his wealth in wild living. ^{14} After he had spent everything, there was a severe famine in that whole country, and he began to be in need. ^{15} So he went and hired himself out to a citizen of that country, who sent him to his fields to feed pigs. ^{16} He longed to fill his stomach with the pods that the pigs were eating, but no one gave him anything.

^{17} "When he came to his senses, he said, 'How many of my father's hired servants have food to spare, and here I am starving to death! ^{18} I will set out and go back to my father and say to him: Father, I have sinned against heaven and against you. ^{19} I am no longer worthy to be called your son; make me like one of your hired servants.' ^{20} So he got up and went to his father.

"But while he was still a long way off, his father saw him and was filled with compassion for him; he ran to his son, threw his arms around him and kissed him.

^{21} "The son said to him, 'Father, I have sinned against heaven and against you. I am no longer worthy to be called your son.'

^{22} "But the father said to his servants, 'Quick! Bring the best robe and put it on him. Put a ring on his finger and sandals on his feet. ^{23} Bring the fattened calf and kill it. Let's have a feast and celebrate. ^{24} For this son of mine was dead and is alive again; he was lost and is found.' So they began to celebrate.

^{25} "Meanwhile, the older son was in the field. When he came near the house, *he heard music and dancing. ²⁶ So he called one of the servants and asked him what was going on. ²⁷ 'Your brother has come,' he replied, 'and your father has killed the fattened calf because he has him back safe and sound.'*

²⁸ "*The older brother became angry and refused to go in. So his father went out and pleaded with him. ²⁹ But he answered his father, 'Look! All these years I've been slaving for you and never disobeyed your orders. Yet you never gave me even a young goat so I could celebrate with my friends. ³⁰ But when this son of yours who has squandered your property with prostitutes comes home, you kill the fattened calf for him!'*

³¹ "'*My son,' the father said, 'you are always with me, and everything I have is yours. ³² But we had to celebrate and be glad, because this brother of yours was dead and is alive again; he was lost and is found.'*"

In this story, the son took his inheritance while his father was living. Think about that for a while. A son telling his father, "I do not want to wait until you are dead to get my inheritance. I want my inheritance now." In a culture where one had to wait until death before gaining an inheritance, much like most all cultures now, this son says I want my inheritance now. It is almost like saying, "I wish you were dead so that I could get my inheritance." Or, "I cannot wait until you are dead, I want my inheritance now." Either way, his father was more than likely hurt, disappointed, or deeply betrayed. However, after the son had a desire to return to his father's home, he did not even have time to deliver his well-rehearsed speech. The father was so ready and willing to forgive and to have his son back, that he ran out after him, greeted him with a kiss, put a garment over him, and had a welcome home party. His father forgave him.

Despite what we have done, where we have gone in this life, or who we have wronged, our God is willing to forgive us and forget all that we have done. How good it is to know that there is a God who is willing to do all of this? Who is willing to bypass all I have done just so that He can have the relationship with me that He had intended from the beginning? There is nothing you have done that God will not forgive.

==PAUSE==

("GOD, HELP ME TO SEE WHERE I HAVE WRONGED YOU")

If you find it necessary, please feel free to re-read this chapter. And remember to "pause", take some time, and soak it in prior to moving on to Chapter 6, where you will be reading about "God is Redeemer".

Chapter 6

God is Redeemer

Preacher's Kid (PK): *The child of a preacher. The PK is usually held to higher standards by church members. This expectation usually places undue stress on PKs. In some cases, PKs choose not to live up to these expectations.*

Forgiveness: *A very important element in the Christian walk. Not holding anger or resentment helps to build a relationship with each other and with God.*

Redeemed: *To be brought back into a relationship with God after separation due to sin.*

Satan: *One of the Archangels whose name was once Lucifer. He was created by God and later rebelled against God. He became known as the Devil or Satan. He seeks to destroy man, whom God loves.*

Walk: *When a Christian uses this word, he or she is referring to their day-to-day life as a Christian. This is usually said in relation to the challenges with which Christians are faced as we live in this world.*

Light: *In the Christian lingo, the word "light" is used to symbolize that which is good and right.*

Darkness: *This word is used in Christianity to refer to that which is bad and evil.*

Blood of Jesus Christ or Blood of the Lamb: *This refers to the sacrifice that Jesus made for us. It refers to His death, in stead of us, which was necessary for the payment for our sin.*

Atone: *To compensate, to pay the penalty for. Christians believe that the death of Jesus Christ pays the penalty for, or compensates for, the sins we have committed.*

> *Galatians 2:20 I have been crucified with Christ and I no longer live, but Christ lives in me. The life I now live in the body, I live by faith in the Son of God, who loved me and gave himself for me.*

Cynthia was a student of mine. Of course, her name was not really Cynthia. I am just using that name to protect her identity. Cynthia was a preacher's kid (PK). She grew up all her life attending church, bible studies, and other church activities. As is the case with most PKs, she was seen as the model kid.

For many years she lived and did what was expected of her. Then the time came when her life did not resemble the life she had grown up living. When I first saw her, she was sitting in my class dressed and groomed in a gothic style. All her clothing was black. Black eye liner, mascara, and eye shadows deeply contrasted her almost lily-white skin. Her fingernails were black, boots and socks were a matching black. Her hair was also entirely colored black except for the half inch or so at the roots that indicated her hair was previously another color.

Over many years I had encountered many individuals who dressed similarly. However, there was something about Cynthia that was different. Something about the way she carried herself led me to believe she was scared, lost, and searching for purpose. After a somewhat lengthy conversation with her, she disclosed her belief that she had done too much wrong for God to forgive her. As she spoke about some of the experiences she had been involved with during her short life, I thought of the scripture where we are reminded that there is nothing that can separate us from the love of God.

You may be asking, "What does Cynthia's story have to do with redemption?" Here it goes: Cynthia prayed that she would be forgiven; she prayed that God would accept her back into the "family". However, she still felt distant. She felt as though she was forgiven, but she was viewing God from a distance and not in the personal and intimate way she had before. Immediately I remembered the story about the prodigal son that was told in the previous chapter. Right then and there, we prayed. I told God that she was reaching out to Him. That she was just outside to gate to the house, -- using a metaphor of course -- asking to come in. And I asked God to go out and get His daughter who was just outside the gate, begging to be let back in.

The next time I saw Cynthia was the following week in class. Reality is I did not recognize her. I thought this was a new student in the class, or a student who had been on the roster and not attending. She had taken off all the black makeup, changed the shoes and socks, redid her hair. Over the weekend she had gone back to church with her father. Most important she knew, believed and felt she had been forgiven and was back in relationship with God. She had been redeemed.

When we live our lives in a manner that is contrary to that which God has intended, we are drawn away from our creator, God. Sin separates us from God when we are drawn away from God toward things that do not look like God. For example, when someone falls into the sin of adultery, that path leads away from God. Adultery hurts and does not show love toward those involved. The lack of love here is contrary to God's command to: *"love one another as I have loved you"* (John 3:34). Sin, as we saw earlier, shows and demonstrates disrespect toward God by choosing to follow and obey Satan the destroyer, rather than the God who created and loves us.

Many have argued that the reason God has all these rules is because He does not want us to have any fun. The truth is quite the contrary. God has given us these guidelines so that we can have fun and not get hurt. Again, using the example of adultery, we can just imagine for a while the consequences that come as a result of engaging in sexual intercourse outside the union of marriage. Children growing up without parents, the financial burden that usually stays with the custodial parent, sexually transmissible diseases, and the emotional hurt that occurs to the person left behind are but a few of the notable results. When sex is experienced outside of a committed and binding relationship that God has ordained, the sexual act can be very hurtful. However, when done as God has ordained, it is a good thing without any bad consequences. It is for our good that God has established guidelines.

Ultimately living a life in sin or contrary to the will of God leads to death. As said earlier, sin leads us to be separate from God. God is the only one who can give eternal life. When we live a life separate from God, it is then not possible to have life. The life lived in sin will eventually lead to death. Romans 3:23, in the King James Version of the Bible, puts it this way, *"The wages of sin is death…"* Put another way, the natural consequences of sin in one's life is death. The death spoken of here is one from which there is no resurrection to life. It is from this state of being on "death row" that we are redeemed. Brought back into the "troop". Brought back into a relationship with God.

==PAUSE==

("GOD, HELP ME TO UNDERSTAND THE HARMFUL CONSEQUENCES OF SIN IN MY LIFE")

> *1 John 1:7 But if we walk in the light, as he is in the light, we have fellowship with one another, and the blood of Jesus, his Son, purifies us from all sin.*

When you are redeemed, you are brought back into a relationship with God. The natural question would now be, how is this made possible? This is all made possible — here is another phrase we use that will need some explanation — "through the blood of Jesus Christ". In Chapter 1 we read John 1:1 where it says that God and the Word existed in the beginning. Later, in that same chapter under Verse 14 it says, *"The Word became flesh and made his dwelling among us. We have seen his glory, the glory of the one and only Son, who came from the Father, full of grace and truth.".* This is what we refer to as, *"God Incarnate"* or God made flesh. God came in the form of man. This man we all know as Jesus the Christ, or Jesus the Messiah.

Jesus came to this earth, was born of a virgin, and lived His entire existence as fully human. He experienced the entire range of emotions just as we do. The book of Hebrews 4:15 says, *"For we do not have a high priest who is unable to empathize with our weaknesses, but we have one who has been tempted in every way, just as we are—yet he did not sin".* He experienced the same things we experienced, but without sinning. He experienced prejudice just as we do. He experienced pain and hurt just as we do. *"He was despised and rejected by humanity, a man of suffering, and familiar with pain. Like one from whom people hide their faces he was despised, and we held him in low esteem"* (Isaiah 53:3).

Why would the Jesus come to the earth and put Himself through such things? Simply put, love. John 3:16 explains, *"For God so loved the world that he gave his one and only son, that whoever believes in him shall not perish but have eternal life."* As a demonstration of His love to all of us, Jesus, also known as the Word, came to this earth, became a human being, experienced life as a human being, and died to atone for our sins. When Jesus the Messiah (or Savior) died, the penalty for sin was put out of the way. There was a reprieve on your execution. You were pardoned, acquitted, excused, absolved of all wrong doing. Sin no longer holds you in bondage, and you are then free to go back to God. That is, sin no longer stands between you and God and because of the death of Jesus the Christ you can now enter a relationship with God. You, upon entering that relation with God, are **REDEEMED**. Redeemed from sin and Satan's way into a relationship with God. You are brought into the "family" of God. Brought back into a relationship with God and out of the influence of Satan.

==PAUSE==

THINK A WHILE ABOUT WHAT YOUR LIFE WILL BE LIKE WHEN REDEEMED.

God is the Redeemer. He is our redeemer. He is your redeemer. God has created you so that He can have a relationship with you. Sin entered the world and entered your life. Since sin entered your life, your relationship with your father has suffered because you have strayed from Him. God loved you so much that the "Word" became flesh, came to the earth and died to remove that penalty of death that hung over your head. Remember the natural consequences of a life lived contrary to the will of God is death (Romans 6:23). When you accept this sacrifice that paid the penalty on your behalf, you are immediately acquitted of all charges and do not need to die for your own sins. Jesus our Savior already suffered and died for you. With sin and the penalty for sin removed, you are now free to return to God as He welcomes you into a life with Him. You are then **reconciled** to God and **redeemed** from sin and Satan. You are a child of the Living God.

This is much like a child who had been abducted, from his or her parents by kidnappers or traffickers. The parent goes after the child and pays whatever ransom necessary for the freedom of their beloved child. After the ransom has been paid, the parents return home with the child. The ransom for the child has been paid. The child has been returned to the parent, and the child has been redeemed from the kidnappers or traffickers and reconciled to the parents.

==PAUSE==

DO I WANT TO BE REDEEMED?

If you find it necessary, please feel free to re-read this chapter. And, remember to "pause", take some time and soak it in prior to moving on to Chapter 7, where you will be reading about "Jesus Is Savior".

Chapter 7
Jesus is Savior

Salvation: *Deliverance from the consequence of sin, which is death. This is made possible because of the death of Jesus.*

Savior: *For Christians, Savior always refers to Jesus. These words are used interchangeably. When we say Savior, we all understand that this always refers only to Jesus.*

Jesus Saves: *A term referring to the work that Jesus came to this world to do. It also is understood that Jesus is the only one who saves, and that salvation comes only through Him.*

> *Acts 4:12 Salvation is found in no one else, for there is no other name under heaven given to mankind by which we must be saved.*

Thus far you have learned that you were created by God to have a close and personal relationship with Him. Sin entered your life and sin led you away from God and the relationship He intended. The sin that separated you from God also brought with it the penalty of death that was paid by Jesus the Messiah. When He sacrificed Himself for you, that debt was paid and upon acceptance of His paying that debt for you, all sins have been forgiven. You have been redeemed and are now free to follow God's way of life that leads to peace, joy, and an intimate relationship with Him.

In this chapter, you will look at Jesus as the only one who saves. Many today preach a false doctrine that states that there are many ways or paths toward salvation or toward God the Father. This is simply not the truth, as you will see.

As you journey into this segment of Christian belief, there are a few things that will be helpful to remember and keep in mind. You learned that God is the one who created all things. He designed and put together all the parts so that everything He created would function in the manner He designed it. Also, everything He designed and created works together in a sort of elaborately choreographed dance where each part of the creation works separate from the other, yet is still dependent on each other.

God alone has the "blueprint" of creation. As much as man believes he knows so much, man is only scratching the surface. It reminds me of the anecdote where man challenged God that he — man — could also make a human being, just like God did. God accepted the challenge and took dirt and made man. Man then took dirt and was about to show God he could also make man. God suddenly stopped man from going any further. Man asked, "God why did you stop me?" God said, "First you must make your own dirt." *Smile.*

God is the ultimate and there is no one like Him. God is the Creator and there is no other. Therefore, because God is ultimate and there is no power that can match or that can even come close to that of God — Sovereign — then He has the sole authority to decide what is right and what is wrong. He has the sole authority to decide by what manner we approach Him or come into relationship with Him and under what circumstances He will forgive sin. He will decide what price He will accept for the sins we have committed. If a human king can dictate that any one coming into his presence must kneel and give respect, then how much more can the King of the Universe decide? God, therefore, has supreme, absolute, and sovereign authority to do whatever He wants, whenever He wants, and however He wants. He makes the rules out of love for us.

==PAUSE==

("GOD, HELP ME TO GRASP THE BREADTH OF YOUR AUTHORITY")

The issue of God's sovereign and absolute rule, by far, creates the greatest challenge for humanity. We naturally want to make our own decisions and do what we believe to be right. We want to "chart our own course", make our own decisions. We want independence. The acceptance of God's sovereign and absolute rule in one's life is critical to understanding and living in obedience to the will of God.

God made man. And in man's imperfection God knew man would sin and would need a Savior — much like any parent who knows their child. If you are a parent you know which child took the cookie, which one spilled the milk and did not clean it up, which one is lying. God knew we would need a savior and set in motion the plan for our salvation. In the book of 1 Peter 1:18-20, Peter says, *"For you know that it was not with perishable things such as silver or gold that you were redeemed from the empty way of life handed down to you from your ancestors, but [you were redeemed] with the precious blood of Christ, a lamb without blemish or defect. He was chosen before the creation of the world…"* The words "you were redeemed" have been included to help with the clarity of the passage.

It is not riches or idols or other people that redeem us; it is only "the precious blood of Christ, the Lamb" that redeems us from sin. This plan to redeem humanity from sin was hatched "before the creation of the world". There is a great plan in action that much of humanity are not aware of. There is a great purpose for our lives and God is always involved.

The great God who created everything, who also put together the plan for the redemption of humanity, dictates how the plan will unfold. He only has the authority to determine how individuals will come to Him because it is His plan.

The first step in the plan can be found in John 1:1, 14. It says, *"In the beginning was the Word and the Word was with God and the Word was God"*. In Verse 14 we see that the Word who was God, *"became flesh and made his dwelling among us"*. Verse 14 also gives testimony that *"… We have seen his glory, the glory of the one and only Son, who came from the Father, full of grace and truth."* He was seen and His works were witnessed.

It is through Jesus the Christ only that we have salvation. Speaking of Jesus, the Christ, *"Salvation is found in no one else, for there is no other name under heaven given to mankind by which we must be saved"* (Acts 4:12).

There are many scriptures through which Jesus attests that He is the only way to God, the only means by which we can be saved, that He is the savior and that it is only through Him that anyone has the opportunity for salvation.

Take as much time as you need to go through the following scriptures:

> **John 14:6** Jesus answered, "I am the way and the truth and the life. No one comes to the Father except through me.
>
> **Matthew 11:27-28** "All things have been committed to me by my Father. No one knows the Son except the Father, and no one knows the Father except the Son and those to whom the Son chooses to reveal Him. "Come to me, all you who are weary and burdened, and I will give you rest."
>
> **Isaiah 43:11** "I, even I, am the Lord, and there is no savior besides Me.
>
> **Hosea 13:4** "Yet I have been the Lord your God Since the land of Egypt; And you were not to know any god except Me, for there is no savior besides Me."
>
> **Psalms 3:8** "From the Lord comes deliverance. May your blessing be on your people.";
>
> **Romans 1:16** "For I am not ashamed of the gospel, because it is the power of God that brings salvation to everyone who believes: first to the Jew, then to the Gentile."
>
> **1 John** 2:2 "He is the atoning sacrifice for our sins, and not only for ours but also for the sins of the whole world."

Luke 2:11 "Today in the town of David a Savior has been born to you; He is the Messiah, the Lord."

Galatians 2:20 "I have been crucified with Christ and I no longer live, but Christ lives in me. The life I now live in the body, I live by faith in the Son of God, who loved me and gave Himself for me."

Hebrews 7:25 "Therefore He is able to save completely those who come to God through Him, because He always lives to intercede for them."

Romans 3:23-24 "For all have sinned and fall short of the glory of God, and all are justified freely by His grace through the redemption that came by Christ Jesus."

Ephesians 1:7 "In Him we have redemption through His blood, the forgiveness of sins, in accordance with the riches of God's grace."

Hebrews 12:2 "Fixing our eyes on Jesus, the pioneer and perfecter of faith. For the joy set before Him He endured the cross, scorning its shame, and sat down at the right hand of the throne of God."

Romans 5:10 "For if, while we were God's enemies, we were reconciled to Him through the death of His Son, how much more, having been reconciled, shall we be saved through His life!"

Hebrews 5:9 "And, once made perfect, He became the source of eternal salvation for all who obey Him."

Welcome back. I truly pray that as you were reading the scriptures from the Bible, God was saying something to you. Even if it was as simple as assuring you that He is your Savior. You have just looked at some of the many scriptures that identify the Word who became flesh, Jesus the Christ, as the

Savior of the world. It is by Him, Jesus Christ, and by Him only, that we can be saved. He is the way to salvation. There is no other power by which we can be saved. No one else has the power to accomplish this or the authority to extend salvation to any of us. Take some time now and prayerfully think through the things that are on your mind now.

==PAUSE==

("GOD, HELP ME PROCESS WHAT I HAVE JUST READ")

If you find it necessary, please feel free to re-read this chapter. And remember to "pause", take some time and soak it in.

Conclusion

After reading this text, my hope is that you have grown to understand just a bit more about the person who created and loves you. My prayer is that through your reading, the veil is being removed, and you are beginning to see what has been hidden under that veil for much of history. I pray that who has been unveiled is the God who created and loves you. The God who, though hurt and disappointed, still loves. The God who loves so much that He sent His son to die so that you can be reconciled to Him in a true, loving relationship. I also pray that by now you would have taken a step closer to a relationship with the God who is being unveiled to you.

It really has been a pleasure walking with you through the unveiling of our God. If you found this to be helpful and easy to follow, please feel free to share with others. And may the God of peace, who desires all good for you, continue to bless you with all understanding and wisdom in His word as you continue to seek Him and His will, AMEN.

Glossary

Adam: *The first man created by God. He was created from dirt.*

Amen: *It is a word said by all Christians at the end of every prayer. It symbolizes our agreement with what was said during the prayer.*

Atone: *To compensate, to pay the penalty for. Christians believe that the death of Jesus Christ pays the penalty for, or compensates for, the sins we have committed.*

Bible: *It is believed that the Bible is comprised of many different sacred writings. Each of these sacred writings were written by men who were inspired by God over the period of centuries. This is the book that defines the Christian's way of life.*

Blood of Jesus Christ or Blood of the Lamb: *This refers to the sacrifice that Jesus made for us. It refers to His death, in stead of us, which was necessary for the payment for our sin.*

Christ: *Messiah or savior. It is a title given to Jesus as He is the savior of humanity. Christians use this title when referring to Jesus.*

Christian: *One who has accepted the death of Jesus the Christ as payment for sins and has also accepted Him as his or her Lord and Master. This person is also in covenant to live a life that is in obedience to God.*

Church: *Comes from the Greek work Ekklesia meaning called out ones. Referring to the people or followers of the Christian God. This word "Church" does not refer to a "Church Building" but to the people.*

Creation Week: *The segment of time within which God the Creator,* *created all things. This period is divided into 7 segments identified in the Bible as days. As there are 7 days in which God created, this segment of time became known as Creation Week.*

Creator: *Refers to the one who created all things. The Christian refers to this person as God.*

Darkness: *This word is used in Christianity to refer to that which is bad and evil.*

Eve: *The first woman created by God. She was created from the rib of her husband Adam.*

Forgiveness: *A very important element in the Christian walk. Not holding anger or resentment helps to build a relationship with each other and with God.*

Garden of Eden: *The place where God put Adam and Eve to live after he created them.*

God: *The one who has always existed. The one who created everything that exists. Without beginning or end. He is the most powerful being in existence anywhere.*

Jesus: *the common name that was given to the Messiah or Savior when He was born. It is the common name given to God when He lived in the flesh. Christians use this name in reference to the Messiah.*

Jesus Saves: *A term referring to the work that Jesus came to this world to do. It also is understood that Jesus is the only one who saves, and that salvation comes only through Him.*

Light: *In the Christian lingo, the word "light" is used to symbolize that which is good and right.*

Live your life for Christ: *Living in obedience to everything God says.*

	Living a life in total submission to God.
Living Thing:	*Any organism that has been "birthed", grows, feeds, has the ability to reproduce, and eventually dies.*
Lord:	*Title given to God as Master of all.*
Messiah:	*From the Hebrew language, the Messiah refers to the promised deliverer of the Jewish nation prophesied in the Hebrew sacred writings. The Christian believes the word Messiah is the title of the one who is the promised deliverer of all who seeks delivery. Jesus is a common name of God who became man. Jesus is regarded by Christians as the Messiah or Savior of the Hebrew prophecies and the savior of humanity.*
Preacher's Kid (PK):	*The child of a preacher. The PK is usually held to higher standards by church members. This expectation usually places undue stress on PKs. In some cases, PKs choose not to live up to these expectations.*
Redeemed:	*To be brought back into a relationship with God after separation due to sin.*
Salvation:	*Deliverance from the consequence of sin, which is death. This is made possible because of the death of Jesus.*
Satan:	*One of the Archangels whose name was once Lucifer. He was created by God and later rebelled against God. He became known as the Devil or Satan. He seeks to destroy man, whom God loves.*
Savior:	*For Christians, Savior always refers to Jesus. These words are used interchangeably. When we say Savior, we all understand that this always refers only to Jesus.*
Scriptural references:	*This is an example of a notation that shows a specific*

	part of the Bible to which we are referring. For example, John 1:2 refers to the first chapter in the book of John and the second verse.
The Serpent:	*Symbolic reference to Satan. First referenced in the book of Genesis as the one who tempted Eve.*
Tree of Knowledge of Good and Evil:	*A symbolic or literal tree from which God forbade Adam and Eve from taking its fruit.*
Walk:	*When a Christian uses this word, he or she is referring to their day-to-day life as a Christian. This is usually said in relation to the challenges with which Christians are faced as we live in this world.*
Word of God:	*Is a reference to Jesus and, in some cases, a reference to the words he has spoken.*

www.simplicityofthegospel.org

www.ingramcontent.com/pod-product-compliance
Lightning Source LLC
Chambersburg PA
CBHW030138100526
44592CB00011B/951